Words from a Stranger

Miriah Lewis

Presentation by *BookLeaf Publishing*

Web: www.bookleafpub.com

E-mail: info@bookleafpub.com

ISBN: 9789357618540

First edition 2022

*I'd like to dedicate this one to the love that
almost was and still could be.*

ACKNOWLEDGEMENT

Yo, shouts out to my great friend Mariah, aka Mari, aka PIE. This was a journey we embarked on together and I'm happy to have done it with you.

PREFACE

As stated in the description, I really needed a place for my thoughts and feelings to come together outside of my head. Sometimes, one just needs to get right with oneself and this society as a whole seems to be lacking the skillset to do so successfully. These poems are a composition of thoughts that come to me often enough to put them on paper. Typically, I'm daydreaming of my future life with my lover but also about people I care about, the beauty in our world, and the struggles that are inevitable in a life on Earth. My imagination has the space and time to run millions of miles per minute. Sometimes, talking things out with other people doesn't get to a resolve. So, I decided my way of speaking with me is through written word. These pages are reflections of my past thoughts, or feelings that couldn't be worked out in my head and thus, they are here now for the world to consume. Scary stuff, but all in the hopes that someone else can see me and maybe, see themselves in me too.

Sunshine in Autumn

There's nothing quite as
beautiful as
sunrise or sunset during autumn.

Orange and yellow leaves
swing round and round in the chilly wind
dancing intertwined
The rays' light shifts,
in synchronicity
piercing through every nook and crevice
they might find.

Fall always fancies
the idea of a fresh start
while leaving the year's first half
behind.

A warm cup of Joe accompanies me
to the porch,
where I gather my thoughts.

I take a beat to catch the breeze
as I breathe in deep,
soak in the shine between the clouds
and think..

We always seem to
forget how
lovely the crisp air feels
after those short
but brutal months
in nonstop heat.

Aberdeen

How humbling she is;

She who stretches as far as the eye can see.

Looking at her shows me just how small I am in
the shadow of her vastness.

Her many shades of blue wrinkle and wave.

How peaceful a sight;

especially knowing just how vengeful she can
be.

Green & Purple

Your favorite colors are present in so many
things
that it's SO hard not to visualize you positively
far and wide.

In the trees, the leaves.
Along city streets.
In affluent cafes & lodgings.
On the train ride into work.
In all of my favorite salads.
(That one parking lot we frequented.)
Amongst all the contemporary fashion, too.

Not that I mind...

Being reminded of you is perhaps one of
the highest quality sensations I've
EVER experienced.
I've had some time to think about
just how much your favorite colors mean to me.

Purple feels like
Royalty;
You and I encased in a
sleek, silk-lined, faux-fur throw

while cozying up to the fireside.
It excites like winning the royal treatment in a
historic museum;
getting to see works normally hidden from the
public's view.
It even feels soft after I blow up,
still receiving your grace, bringing me peace as
you do.

Green feels like
The woodland; particularly the Colorado pines
who hold their luster all year long.
Evergreen, that's never-ending.
Being safe & secure,
having the openness to be wrong,
possessing the freedom to fail,
an opportunity to mature,
and certainly, a partner for bail!
(jk)

Your favorite colors are forthwith mine too.
Solely because they
remind me
of you.

He(art) Gallery

Welcome to my heart,
otherwise known as one's soul.
It's not often I let folks in here.
You are here, though;
so to you, my heart I'll show.

It may not be transcendently beautiful,
but it is authentic & true.
The walls here are coated in a stunning,
glistening dew,
representative of my tears from quondam pain.

The entryways are a bit beaten and bruised;
much like the ego I destroyed
in exchange for
the insight I gained.

Scars within images
are an ode to remembrance;
present on each anamnesis,
living ever-on in the main foyer
as slight keepsakes
of olden days
that delivered me here now,
in this way.

The floor is a delicate fissured marble,
in which the gaps of a crippled past
are now suffused with aquamarine.
That is, the gem that represents the
advancement
of me.

This gallery is
my life's journey.
A combination of old & new,
lay the foundation to
piece me back together again.

Phoenix - A Haiku

Dynamic savvy
A vengeful phoenix rages
betrayed by the flea

Chat with a Stranger

Coffee-bonding is where it starts
where lavender lattes are a shared passion
A simple, but delicate drink
strings two strangers into friendship

Phantom Pen Pal

Hey there, it's me!
I'm that friend you can't see.
The one who can't leg go
of something I don't know.
So I linger here
for centuries.
Waiting and hoping that you set me free.

Hope - A Didactic Cinquain

Hope
Glorious, triumphant
Swimming, flying, riding
Ever so confident
Light

Anticipation

Instead of sweating,
my palms itch.

A nervous jitter travels down my spine,
causing my hands to clench.

To a happy mental place I went;
distracting my mind from the passing of time.

Insomnia

In the dark for hours I spend
time.
Thinking thoughts,
words running
racing
circling
cycling
through and though to no end.

The therapist said,
"consider reading something boring before bed."

After Party: A Lune

Sweaty, salty, sweet
Temperatures and heart rates rise
Electric and alive

I yearn for your touch
My body writhes
Craving

For & With your Love

For your love, I will do anything
With your love I can do everything
For you, I am forever a student
For you, I am always a safe space
With your love I can do everything
With you, I am my best me
For you, I am always a safe space
To me, you are the future
With you, I am my best me
For you, I am forever a student
To me, you are the future
For your love, I will do anything

Quakes

It started with a series of soft rumbles
that rocked, shifted, and pulsated
as they crept through every morsel of my being
Then they turned to turbulent vibrations
And devoured me whole, delivering my soul to
you

Fave Songs - A Pensee Poem

Sweet memories
Fill my soul with energy
The lyrics dance around my head
Keeping you close to me

Heartbreaking Confessions to the Universe

Oh heavenly stars
dear beings up above
Please help me be free
of being in love
"Everything happens for a reason"
in that,
I believe
Question your will, I don't
but good golly, this pain!
I can't take it,
I WON'T
I hate being hated
or envied and such
Honestly it's he I envy
Because I love him so much
Tell me merciful luminaries
Help me understand
Why do I relish him?
Why does my heart so demand?
I feel my you in my body
Intuition says "go slow"
"You can't rush love"
Oh boy, don't I know
I've bested the patience

I've put in the time
Oh dear Universe,
just give me what's mine.

Trust is...

Gold
Stone cold
Black and white
No room for spite
Blind

What a Woman

She is full of fiery passion.
She is the perfect blend of gangsta and grace.
She is as bright as a shooting star.
She is like butter on fresh baked bread.
She is courageous and charming.
She is as grand as the Nile river.
She is formidable like snowy mountain peaks.
She is nurturing and protective.
She is a warrior.
She is the Queen Bee.

Ode to my Dreams

My pleasant dreams, you inspire me to note.
I love the way you drift and float,
Invading my mind tirelessly,
Always wearing that dark coat.

Let me equate you to a stark clover?
You are more freakish, bewildering, and bright.
Light storms whip the twig-lets of October,
autumn-time the days have shifted,
shorter days and longer nights.

How do I love you? Let me count the ways.
I love that you're forever warm and serene.
Wanting for your delicate illumination fills my
days.
My love for you glows sunny green.

Now I must go away with a dazed heart,
Remember my contention whilst we're apart.

A.G.L.O.M.L

Immediately I was smitten.
I think we both were.

It was the last teen year for both of us;
real life adulthood was coming in quick.
I don't believe either of us had any intention
of falling in love forever,
let alone if real feelings would stick.

But oh, did they stick!

Like flies on a trap.
Or lashes on glue..
I attached myself to you, not having a clue.

This love hasn't been easy,
nor has it always been kind.
But it has certainly taught me lessons,
Taught me patience,
Gave me blessings.

This love has taught me that
life means
so much more
when there's someone you care for.

Even more than that,
you are someone I can't live without.
Trust me, I've tried.

And I've much rather died
than to miss another moment,
second,
hour,
minute.
You are the love of my life.
And forever with you is how I'd like to spend it.

All or Nothing: A Triolet

There is no more space to wait
There is no more time for the in-between
There is no rush but it's getting late
There is no more space to wait
It's time to set the record straight
We have everything we need
There is no more space to wait
There is no more time for the in-between

Last Words

Sweet mother Earth,

You have been so good to thee.

You are the giver of life,
to all I know and most I see.

You deserve better.